Vol. 1

DC Poetry Collective

ISBN: 978-0-578-77713-9

To the multitudes who have perished
and the deaths still to come due to COVID-19.
Our hearts and prayers are in our poetry.

Contents

There is no one among men that has not a special failing:
and my failing consists of writing verses.

Po Chu'i (772-846)

Introduction

When asked why there was no poetry among the hundreds of books in the NY Times summer reading list, the Book Review editor responded, "Because nobody reads it."

Dear Fellow Nobodies,

If you are there, which you must be, we poets write to connect with you. Welcome!

It is quite common for poets to join together in small groups to share their work and tone their craft. Occasionally they evolve from a writing forum into a "collective", a sort of family. DC Poetry started as a workshop in 2006 in Washington, DC. I took over as "host" for this group five years ago, and continued with my cast of fellow nobodies to meet weekly at our spot in the National Portrait Gallery, until COVID-19 stopped the world in March, 2020.

At this unique time in history, poetry events have joined the trend to continue "live" on Zoom and similar platforms. One positive result was allowing our small collective to find new friends and contributors outside our area. Certainly the global reach will continue. The alienation caused by COVID-19 has caused poetry to emerge with new urgency and vitality.

Within the diversity of voices in our group, we feel we have much to give you, newcomers or obsessive readers of poetry.

Your comments are most welcome! Please contact me with any inquiries.

Special thanks to Julie Maurer for her great editorial and interior layout skills to pull this together, and to Martin Parker for his cover illustrations and interior layout assistance.

Mark Fishbein, September, 2020
mark@poetwithguitar.com

Dana Gittings

D ana dove into the Washington, DC writing scene to find company and guidance in the sometimes isolating experience of putting pen to paper. She is finalizing a poetry collection called "The Dark Dance" about alcohol misuse, recovery, identity, and desire. The collection explores how a shared thread of compulsivity can link drinking behavior, intimacy, and the almost manic process of healing through the vehicle of writing.

Her work is most heavily influenced by the confessional poets Sylvia Plath and Anne Sexton, though many other poets have had a profound impact on her—such as Margaret Atwood, Melissa Broder, Andrea Gibson, and Sharon Olds. She is inspired by ecopoetics, surrealism, psychoanalytic theory, and spoken word, and likes to experiment with shape and ekphrastic poetry.

Dana enjoys perusing flea markets and used bookstores, long afternoons writing outside or at coffee shops, and analyzing psychological horror films. She works at a national non-profit social science organization. She also maintains an educational blog on alcohol sobriety.

Website: danagittings.com
Blog: somelikeitsober.com
Instagram: @poetryindc

WEB-WEAVER

Wander into the cradle.
Come into my tangles of twine.
Get lost as I close around you.
Tonight, let me sing you to sleep.

Unite with my wine-soaked semblance.
Wilt slow as you lay by my side.
Drink! Let the bottle bind you.
Let its venom reveal you to me.

Where are your dreams?
Let my hard heart hear them.
Let my siren song sear them.
Soon you'll learn to stay with me.

Skirt the slaughter of daylight.
Stay here in the safety of my arms.
Wait 'til your roving eye runs dry.
She fails to wake you out of me.

THE HARVEST

the horn of the body, the sounding call,
the suppertime, the summoning,
   the berries, the honeydew,
   the brimming, the thirst,
     the bowl of the skin, the beckoning snake,
     the rattle's shake, the devil's wake,
       the ready yet, the heady yes,
       the undress, the steady press,

the bite down, the cruel miss,
the focus, the fracas,
   the frequency, the tortured plea,
   the unashamed, the burrowed bee,
     the crack of lightning through the core,
     the kill, the cleansing,
       the water, water, water flow,
       the deep steep of the bodily know,

the moon's pull, the blood-full,
the she-wolf, the sorceress,
   the red cave, the fruit fist,
   the lioness, the harvest,
     the wheat field, the grain,
     the sound of grunt work in the rain,
       the baker's biscuits, the final flourish,
       the overfull, the push, the pull,

       and the sinking, sinking, sinking
       back to dough.

DALLIANCE

I walk
straight
into you
on the wet
street
stunned
in the shock
of a cigarette
cloud
blind
but starved
I beckon
your trail
of smoke
and with one
deep
breath
drag
you down
to the filter
never l
    e
     t
      y
     o
       u
         g
          o

THE DRINK

you're always there with a wink
a nudge toward numbing my lowering lows
and you know
if you seize my spine
if you twist just right

my eyes will glaze over
my arms go limp
until I slump down at the trough
plunged into the puddle
of your mean-spirited sweat
your hot-blooded heat
your winning smile

and I'm stuck
pinned to the ground
with every sick
stupefying put-down
you can come up with
to keep me here

BELOW THE BELT

As the dust breeds in our hideout
between the hemispheres,
I invoke your living ghost:

a journey through time
and a far-off place,
a casting off and a reeling in,
the ship that sailed with the heat
rising off our backs,
a jaguar and a fish out of water,
two rivers and one raw seam,
running shallow, reaching deep,
stopping short,

left with a swift hug and a hole
where the heart should be,
weeks later and worlds apart,
nothing but water and sky to bind
our far-flung bodies, plagued
with raw want, a rude awakening,
and sweet, sweet memory,
a circus of vine-ripe, vicious visions
torturing through the mind,

the end of a new beginning,
the shock of an endless thirst,
the nest egg tossed
at a lump sum of nothing,
half a planet,
an empty cup.

APERTURE

I breathe in, in,
slow,
deep,
and I am so full
of me,
catching the last
of the thinning
atmosphere
and it feels
like forever is
on my doorstep
and I
am stretching,
edging
like the sickle
of the moon
and I have made it
I am here
and I am ready now
to fall
with a shuddering
yawn
into the wide
open arms
of the galaxy,
staring into her
shining eyes
that blink once
as I collapse
into a single
spark—

MOON-BOUND

I find you in a dream.
I'm coming home,
burying the hatchet
of an old and dwindling rage—

so many years
after the moon broke,
the stars searching blind for their places
in the sky.

You look at me
for a spell,
blankly staring,
a thicker book than broken hearts can read.

The full circle of time apart
ebbs over your body
as you roll away, facing
what I can't see in your eyes—

the flesh of years
tendered loose
as we marched on
each day and each night,

one life and one death,
two halves of a once
so warmly lit
whole.

Elizabeth Black

Elizabeth is a resident of Arlington, Virginia. She worked as a nurse for forty years in Mexico and Northern Virginia in the fields of rural health, intensive care and psychiatry. She currently serves as a regional master naturalist in Arlington. She is a painter and printmaker and taught art as adjunct faculty at The George Washington University and Trinity University. She is the recipient of numerous art awards including a Fulbright Scholarship and her art is found in several private and public collections.

Her passions for art, art history, the natural world and world cultures have led Elizabeth to travel the world. Although she is a latecomer to writing poetry, Elizabeth acknowledges a lifelong love for poetry, a love she is driven to explore. Her poetry has been published in *Blythe Spirit, Bottle Rockets, Frogpond, Heron's Nest, Modern Haiku, The Northern Virginia Review,* and *Verse Virtual.*

Elizabeth holds a BA and BFA from The University of Michigan and a MA and MFA from The George Washington University.

TWILIGHT IN THE COMPANY
OF OTHERS

I stop to watch
late September
chimney swifts gather
    scatter
    regather
ever greater numbers
       soar and   dart
all directions
    against
       the giant autumn sky

each return
brings a greater mass of swifts
more than a thousand swarm
circle counterclockwise
in darkening sky

    in choreographed precision
       whirl the opposite direction

disappear as a mist like a   d r i f t i n g   cloud
    a world of orange and pink

biology summons   the birds return
flying round and round
an ever tighter circle
    wild and ecstatic
    mystic dervish dancers
    whirling
    faster and faster
until they funnel
and
d
r
o
p
in the old trash chimney in
ones
pairs
and more
their descent
too fast
for my eyes to follow
until
not a single swift
remains in sight

    I am left alone
        the full moon blazing
            to walk home
            my shadow   following

AMERICAN TOADS

they come from forest and wet lands
hundreds hopping from hibernation
to the old pond baring earth's minerals
in musky skin shades—orange brown

yellow gray   they come warty bodies
loping bounding short back legs pressing
to slippery banks fertile breeding water
greening duck weed and bladderwort

they come spring rain awakening
the annual sex orgy as males mount
females and males mount males front legs
grabbing from behind spilling sperm

long strings of floating eggs waiting
they come send waves into the pond
waves into the world—a toad choir sings
loud and hypnotic a hallelujah chorus

MOVING ON

awakened
by a stream of rain
    I went to hear
           the creek run wild   overflow
                      its banks and eddy past
trees   invade the meadow where it flooded
      to stillness   drown holes of moles and fox
      burst the cells
          of viburnum and redbud

          I watched
          narrow sedge leaves and jointed grass   uproot
          flash past on the water surface   drag on roots

          I stood
on a dry boulder island watched
      the sizzle of bubbles rushing
           to undercut trees   flush the earth and stones
                      sweep trapped crayfish
                and snakes into the water
                 eroding digesting
                    pouring remnants
down miles of current   to the bay where oysters
          and crabs in frenzy fed on the river detritus

the pressured journey disquieted me
as I tucked a snag of graying hair behind my ear

behind me spires of ancient oaks stood firm

PURIFICATION RITES

I stood on the roadside
where a dead doe lay. Pinched
my nose. Breathed death.
Above me twelve vultures
teetered   sniffed   circled.

Animals, maybe a fox
or coyote, chewed the carcass
tore a foreleg free. Flies and
larval progeny buzzed
the carcass, tasted its afterlife.

Plenty flesh remained
for the noble carrion
weaving and waiting for me
to leave. Not like buzzards
at the Towers of Silence

where I watched Parsi
Indians leave bodies —
hosts for disease and decay
invitation to corpse eating

birds who came to pick
the rotting flesh clean
purify life's debris and
leave bleached bones
leaching back to earth.

I walked on. Left the dead deer leaving
the vultures to swallow death.

MOTHER

I take her dry body
pound it   sift it
back to dust
mix it with grandmother's
crushed vessel
her inert grit
adding strength.

I wash the generations
soak the earth
with tears
make clay
remold it spinning
on an axis
forming a bowl

forming a womb
to hold life
of ancient women
who formed me
and keep
as duty
ontological order.

THE BROWN SPIDER

He's a liberated man.
Crouched below the porch
light where he crochets
his silk doily—
an intricate pattern
a spiraled whorl
that keeps him busy
as he dreams
the lovely woman
dressed in white
the moth who flutters
by the lamp each evening
with her sultry legs.
I thought her overweight
too big not his taste
not his type of catch

but who am I
to judge?
She landed trapped
in his sticky net
sputtered and flailed.
He doomed her
powdered wings subdued
her feathered feelers
with his tinsel strength.
His gossamer filaments
condemning her
as he ambled
to enshroud his prey
bind her like a mummy.
A man
not so liberated after all.

CALL AND RESPONSE

late night
starless and black
a loon calls his mate
from the lake's wide water

where are you
    where are you

she answers him

I am here
    I am here

back and forth—
the same question
the same answer
    year after year after century

I sound my call
listen for your response
waiting for the hollow echo
    of my belly
        waking my heart
            that longs to belong

Julie Maurer

*J*ulie Maurer discovered her love of writing in midlife after working in the corporate world and later as a professional organizer, yoga instructor, massage therapist and facilitator of Scott Kiloby's *Living Inquiries.* Now when someone asks her what she does for a living she is happy to say "writer."

Recently she has begun exploring poetry and enjoying the creative freedom she finds in this way of expressing herself, which is very different from the more structured requirements of prose.

She lives in Rockville, Maryland, with her husband, Jeff, and her American Eskimo dog, Juno. Whenever

possible, she loves to take long walks with both of them or, in the days before COVID-19 and hopefully again soon, go into Washington, DC, to share Free Hugs on the National Mall.

Julie is the author of *Embracing the Unknown: One Woman's Radical Decision to Turn Her Life Over to the Universe and the Amazing Transformation that Follows.*

To find out more about her book or to read her articles or blog, visit her website at **www.juliemariamaurer.com.**

TELL ME

Tell me your story.
Not your successes,
your failures,
your victories
and defeats,
nor the gains and losses
in the battles of your life.

Tell me your story.
I want to know
your deepest desire.
The one that pulses
in your every cell,
echoes in your dreams,
will not let you rest
until you unchain your soul
from what you have been told
you should want.

Tell me your story
about this longing
you can't quite name,
this mysterious hunger
that refuses to be satisfied
in the world of win and lose.

Stand naked to yourself
in this quest for your Truth.
Find it and you find
everything.

Tell me your story.

TWO PATHS

Inspired by "The Road Not Taken"
by Robert Frost

Two paths diverged
in a yellow home –
and grateful I could not travel both,
though I looked down yours
as far I could
to where it bent you
in its undergrowth,
from which you never emerged.

I chose the other, much more fair
though not without its thorns.
In the end it had the better claim,
though in a way
the results are the same
and death comes in many forms.

I shall recall this with a sigh –
you taught me much
by your descent.
We diverged – you and I,
the same and yet so different.

LOOM OF LIFE

At first so faint
we do not hear
the click and clack,
yet year by year

the shuttle threads
unceasingly
through vines and briars
and life's debris.

Round dreams that died
and dreams bestowed,
from vows we've made
to vows we broke,

strand by strand
hard lessons weave
a net of grace,
sweet mercy's face.

Until we find
there is entwined
in warp and weft
a warm embrace

to catch our souls
and tightly bind
in filaments
of love designed

to spin us out
and spin us in,
to set us free
again, again.

TURTLE

Even for a stuffed toy
you were pretty quiet.

I don't recall you
ever saying a word,
even in my darkest moments.

But your stitched-on smile
never wavered
as you unfailingly offered
undivided attention,
unconditional love
and steadfast companionship
to a little girl
who so often felt
scared and alone.

Fifty years later,
you still offer your beautiful smile
whenever I remember to
glance your way.

But my smile back is bittersweet.
The magic is gone,
I have moved on
and you could not follow.

I am so sorry
you are only a toy
and I can no longer pretend.
I miss you, my friend.

MIZERENE

Come one, come all!
Heed the voyeur's call –
step in from the mizerene!
Take your seat in the gladiplex –
prepare to be entertweened!

Viewserve each player carefully
in their chosen flamoglue.
Their proximist emotications
oh so fleshly true!

Grabhold your chance
to vixhartle and garlance.
Everyone is doing it,
so why the heck not you?

Flay them! Slay them!
Endlessly replay them!
Revortle in the mayhem
and give Maximonius his due.

Jollyfind the spectacle,
point out the stone you threw,
but never, ever, *ever* assume
the players are not you.

SACRIFICE

Atop sacred pyramids
Aztecs ripped out
still-beating hearts,
giving their god strength
to raise the sun each day.
Save us, Tonatiuh!

We worship our own gods
with sacrificial rites,
tearing out bits of our hearts,
bearing the pain,
fearing the dark.
Save us, Tonatiuh!

We make ourselves bleed
while we proudly display
the scars of our ignorance,
in the mistaken belief
we cannot rise on our own.
Save us, Tonatiuh!

YES

At first, I resist.
No, not this…
Then I surrender.
Do what you will.

Sparks fly
as I am engulfed
in tumbling embers of emotion.
It hurts, but *yes… yes…*

Finally opening
to burning
is far less painful than trying
to hold the heat at bay,
sequestering it in some dark corner
of my heart
where it lies smoldering,
slowing suffocating me.
Yes…

Now exposed to open air,
I fan the flames
that turn my sorrows
to ash.

No…
Yes…

Keith David Parsons

K eith David Parsons (he/his) is a citizen-poet on the run from the law, yoga aficionado, and a stan without a country. Born in West Virginia, between a crick and a hollar, he lives in Washington, Douglass Commonwealth.

@Kristophanes on Twitter/Facebook
keithdavidparsons on Instagram

GOLDFINCHES

One day it was raining too
humid air kept the avenue exhaust
close to the ground
I was passing nameless glass
with two miles to go
secretaries hurried by
eyes down
but

> in the cornflowers
> in the rain garden
> between sidewalk and street

five goldfinches
were swooping in and out
from the branches of a dwarf ash tree
plucking tiny seeds from
prickly cones one by one

by one
by one

by one

7TH STREET, NW

Street of sensation
and skinned knees!

Go-go blares from the corner
where it overtops Georgia Avenue
Listen! hear the jazz echo
from Black Broadway.

Down street the vast vistas of the Mall
see pink-crowned Women's Marchers
gawk at tourists in matching t-shirts.

Smell the smoky insouciance
the last whiff of the '68 riots
mixed with Irish whiskey tastings
and wet brisket.

Feel it grab you with the dry scratchy hands
of a homeless man praying a blessing
and hold you with the hauteur of Elizabeth Taylor
glancing back over a beer garden.

It trips you while jogging,
you roll, gravel grinding into your flesh,
stumble to the studio bleeding.

But the sun still blasts over the roofline
as though raised by your salutations,
and your leg throbs as you
find your final
shavasana.

PENNSYLVANIA AVENUE, NW

And what song is he singing?
      The street preacher spits into the megaphone
that monkey standing next to you?
      I imagine a cymbal monkey toy, banging away
      to drown out any racial overtones
there's another mask beside you!
      he singsongs another few lines until
      the tune of Masquerade reveals itself.
            Andrew Lloyd Webber might approve
            he wrote Jesus Christ, Superstar, after all.
      What of that mask in Masquerade—
      the mask as fantasy, role play, escape
      there is no escape here.
      The screamer invokes the mask as sin
      concealment, shame, deception.

there's another mask beside you
      And yet, he also proclaims the times
      covering of faces for the Covid crisis
      mask as judgement
      on a corrupt nation.
            He screams from Lafayette Park
            the White House faces his black signs.
            But it is April, George Floyd yet breathes
            the park is yet un-fenced
            protesters yet un-gassed
            un-bruised by rubber bullets
            the President has yet to
            hold a Bible in front of his face.
and what song is he singing?

16TH STREET, NW

The White House was black once
    and blackened in 1812.
A block north, an octagonal cement sarcophagus
    was reborn into a flame of glass,
    like an on-the-nose phoenix,
    down the street from where a friend
    got her first abortion—now condos.
Mary Foote Henderson would be proud:
    her castle mansion thrown down
    for a gated community
    the old gate house stands;
    and the pink palace she built—now beige.
The White House was black once
    and rainbow too—once.
My friend once lived far up-street in the Woodner,
    known for bedbugs and murder.
    Her heat blew out and she had to stay
    at that inn, by that one bodega;
    bad luck perhaps.
Across from the pink palace—now beige
    the Founders tried to upend Greenwich
    with an American Meridian, and
    Malcolm X tried to upend them; in summer
    you may hear the District's largest drum circle.
The White House was black once,
    built by slaves, and Masons.

At All Souls Marion Barry ran for mayor, for life,
     and my friend married a blogger, for life, and
     across the way the Moonies bought a church
     while another was turned into a charter school, and
     a Mason lodge is turning into more condos.
The green of Rock Creek Park
     encroaches on the avenue at intervals,
     and blends with the blue of those tennis courts
     where the Williams sisters play, near
     the consulate where they paint trees white.
Oh 16th Street;
     street of colors, churches and columnar oaks,
     hold your Meridian fast and run for Silver Spring!
The White House was black once,
     now blackened.

HARVARD STREET, NW

It is cool for an August day
overcast clouds clad in mild roiling
their canopy keeping
energy close to the earth
a boy on a bike whips 'round the corner
black bangs flapping.

I can hear on the breeze police
sirens luring us onto the rocks
there was kettling two nights ago
arrests by the plaza
graffiti on the crosswalk
white stripes set off black words.

This morning a protest
after the postmaster general admitted
the removal of sorting machines
depositories and employees
was—for real—to fuck the election
blue lives matter but not blue boxes.

But still the storm is corked
in a vital bottle
of low pressure or false faith
the cinder ceiling of sky
channeling the chaos
into a boy's hair
like the breath of fall, or
breath of the fall, or
both.

MASSACHUSETTS AVENUE, NW

The next year
they planted cornflowers again
I waited
As I walked by with my coffee
    in the morning
      passing nameless glass
As I jogged by
    in the evening
      with two miles to go
I waited
The cornflowers grew
bloomed, crisped, dried
but
when mature, brown
and laden with seeds
they cut off their heads

leaving stalks like burnt skewers

the goldfinches
never came

LKN

L KN (pronounced LaKAN) is a global poet who has shared his poetry in more than 1,600 events in 13 countries – since September 2017.

He was invited to be featured at The History Channel's HistoryCon 2018, The Hong Kong New Music Festival 2018, Singapore Migrant Literature Festival 2019, and in 2020, for Writings on the Wall in England, the award winning US podcast - Poets and Muses, and the Poetry Festival Singapore. LKN also shared his pieces for the Vichar Arts in India, Poets Out Loud in Australia, Winnipeg Writers Festival in Canada, and Jerusalism in Israel.

He has been featured in *The Philippine Daily Inquirer*, *Lifestyle Asia Magazine*, and *Town & Country Magazine*. For radio, TV and digital platforms, LKN was in the Wish 107.5 Bus, EuroTV, and Write Out Loud UK.

He finished as 1st runner-up at the Singapore Poetry Slam in 2019, and was a finalist at the Toronto Poetry Slam 2020 in Canada.

In addition, he was the co-founder of the pioneering international weekly online poetry open mic - We; Poetry Global.

LKN's poetry is part of an anthology in Mumbai, India, and his work was included in an academic publication by Vibal Publishing in the Philippines. LKN is expected to release his debut collection of poetry later in 2020.

AN INKLING OF AN INK, RESTING.

My back, rests calmly on the chair
Reclined, having a gaze of a light moon
Inhaling a welcomed-summer breeze
As it bequeaths, a delightful reprieve
From the arresting tumult of being home
Where my breaths were - apprehended

In the woes of the bleak, swinging feeling
Of my heart skipping, stopping - reading
The many last exhales, and the silence
That follows the tucked white linens
While the wailing is gasped, to wither
In locked toilet doors, and dim street corners

When my strung heart would pause a beat
Just as numbers fly, and letters get buried
When sirens, with blood blinkers, are songs
Last wills, are first read, as resigned poetry
When goodbyes are scratched paintings
Hellos are theatrics, over a zoomed blindness

In skewed photographs of our still-deaths
Of begging, kneeling to a canned-choreography
Of our desolate culinary of selling-out
Bribed, by the momentary-artistry of being numb
Faking. The muses of ends, has arrived
Hanging our fates in an exhibition

Of the artistry of our commercialized-humanity
Found in gunned-clicks of empty shot-alm
Palm, hot-locked, down in an obscure test
To survive from the cent-pest of bureaucracy
That being humane... means to shut our doors
Opening a cracked window, of being no one

Leading our shadows, wondering away
From silver somber-footsteps, under a room
Preps a thumb-question in a numb notification
Tarrying the punned-headlines of our seclusion
Trying to find a reason, while looking - afar

To a shallow-night of p o n d e r e d-stars

TARDE, AHORA... TEMPRANO

Extraño los rocios en nuestros ojos
Cuando tenemos nuestra cama a las cinco
Despierta, llena, pero con miradas carmesi
El sol mira, a las palabras
Mirando en las lineas, habladas
Con una avalancha de verdades tacitas

Permanecer...
en el abrazo de nuestro anhelo
Constante en aprender de es,
y no lo es

Ahora... Todo lo que tenemos nuestros primeros
crepusculos
Sin labios en movimiento,
como jardines aridos
En una noche interminable de silencio
Todo lo que tenemos es un cielo,
con una luna poco profunda
Y las estrellas que parpadean en las nubes
La calma silenciosa del viento del sur

Perdido...
en el dejar ir de nuestro anhelo distancia
Rota de la nesciencia de fue,
y no fue

OH, JOHN

A fire hinged, on a bridged-river ire
Dire beast-bullets in the East, in palletes' liar
Bang! An imperial gang-slang, sang
Clang, a slave spangled-pang, invertedly hang
A behest manifest - a vow of the West
To test-oppressed, a gifted starred-jest
Destiny... will be an ebony-debauchery
Sea. See... believe me; three, isn't a bully

Really...

For them; two's a score on the shore
Roar, more! Ha - Death has no backdoor
But Brownie... money's a price for liberty
For a soiled-colony - hegemony of democracy
Occupy, then buy! "They'll fly", is our alibi
Pacify, comply, and mak'em a no-nigh ally
Let's begin a golden-skin win, with a grin
With a firing-pin of a sin, on a shin-spin

OH, CYAN UNION

Say you'll be with me, always.
Beneath the cerulean waves above,
Under the lit powdered-sky,
Away from God's billion eyes.

Have me marry your coral-fingers
When I behold you in my arms,
Of infinity's most serene care.
I am safe. You are safe. Us, both.

Let me journey to your azure edges.
Through your iridescent shadows,
Your lulling cobalt-depths,
The basking of me... you in a waltz

As we glide through the in-betweens,
The ebonies of our past, blithes
The ivories of our tomorrow, writhes
In the teal-current of NOW.

I surrender, in your full-spectre
Of us, whirling into a tinged-unknown.
Have me... I am your open navy,
Ever so ready, to dive, deeply,

In our hidden respite in each wave.
Those zaffred-hues of your tears,
As you bequeath me a turquoise glance,
And those blue-smiles... is everything.

It is uncertain what fate will give us,
Yet, I'm certain that this vast ocean
Of my wooing; I swoon endlessly,
In the abyss of bliss; you're my paradise,

And I... yours, 'till eternity ends its evermore

SPRING BOX

5AM sang with a pang-bang
A silencer-banter, under
The bright light slight-revolver
On my ear. Hear... I'm still here

Over the joker-corner; a loner
Of our room. Boom! The fume
In a BYE, comes a red-eye sky
Shot, in a slot of a love-not

Silver bullet of a father-figure
Down, came the renown noun
Of my haze-gaze on my blaze
First's of sixes, on ticks' - fixes

Dead! On my bed, I bled by misled
Echoes that bellows HELLOS
Of how a vow can bow. To allow
An excuse of a muse, with a ruse

Railing, reeling the pointing
Aim-blame. Shame the game!
We're a win, 'till the tin-spin
Of your stan-stud dialed-lever

I'm left on a deft bereft
Of a pall-call of a fall
With a sun-gun. I'm done
Being a blast-past that won't last

Over a sulfur-color of a cadaver
Ready to pick, lick a click
Fire! A lamb-liar wants to acquire
But no! Know this, you crow

After this diss of a barrel's kiss
A trigger-clipper of a sinner
Will rise with a locked-vice in sighs
On a cuddle-muzzle. I'll shovel

Grip the tip of a RIP-lip, of a snip-quip
Slide, glide... you, on your 11-side

Now... hide!

TUCK THE TICK TOCK.

Let your heart be still, my dear
In the waiting of the ticking
Let seconds roll in to hours
In the midst of its clicking
Hold your midnight. Firmly
Close to the heart, that can forget
For a while, that being strong
Is to fight. To scream your banners
Holding your battlecry, high
The war of solitude, is not waged
When one screams the truths in lies
Listen to the affinity of abandonment

Let those pauses be your home
The silence... as your great ally
Let the murmurs be rocked-shut
Along with the loud clanking
That bangs your harrowing days
Like calenders were counting
The sixes of your watch
Like you're just a number, in a series
Not knowing how to halt the squeals
Let those shrieks be muted
By the pouting of your own arrow

For now... stay in your hushed
Somber limbo. It's ok. It's alright
Salvation tolls its obscure carillon
In the palms that unexpectedly points
To the refuge of one's quiescence
Cradled, in the words unspoken
There is strength in being quiet

You know... doubt, swings constantly
Like the cogs that wheels your fears
It never holds its own twelve
It shall flail, and let it stay waving
This is not your quietus

Bravery... chimes not at noon
But in the stillness of twilight
Be steadfast on the pulses
As you close its precipitous tapping
Basking in the edges of nothingness
Let hours pass-by, while you wait
You are not less, when you stop
You become more, when you do
Courage is made in surrendering
To admit; I am not ready, not just yet
Till the beat, ticks of YOU
And when it strums the letter - "I"
Keep it. Permit yourself to own it
Wear it in your heart, your soul
For you deserve to say: "I'm here now"
And I am here to stay, with you
Do you know what time that is?!!

When the "I" and the "You", has a "We"
In the middle of OURS

HANDOG NA PAGKAKAHULOG

Pagaspas ay umalpas, sa talampas
Humampas ang matalas na kaskas
Ng Balatik, na nagpabalik-balik
Sa hitik na hagikhik ng pilik
Na gubat na kinagat ng pagkasalat
Nang habagat ay sumibat sa alamat
Haring-ibon ay tinunton ng lupon
Tinugon, nang tinapon ang kapon
Sinimsim ang talim sa kulimlim
Lihim na paglilim, pagkakasakim

Tinulak ang busilak na pakpak
Sinaksak ang paguwak, ng halakhak
Ng bagwis, nang mabilis na kinalis
Ang bihis-litis na pagdadalisdis
Sa tuka, na hinila ang pulang-dila
Sinaksak, sinara ang ngalangala
Baka mahuli ng sisi ang pagsipi
Kaya't may tagpi ang sindi ng hapdi
Di na makagalaw ang dilaw-hiyaw
Hinataw ang bughaw na siglaw
Kamao ang dumapo sa ulong-sulo
Marahuyo ang gulo, ng pagkalilo
Kaya't napiringan ang tangan-kalayaan
Sa tanghalian, bugsuan ng amihan
Ang bumalot, nantakot ang sigalot
Dinakot ang balahibo't buntot
Nilagay ang ibong pinilay, sa hukay
Di pa mamatay, tila'y may inaantay

Ahh... ang iba pang malaya na aguila
Darating sila, madami pa! Pasensya

Mark Fishbein

I have been writing poetry for over fifty years and currently have five collections available on Amazon. I have chosen some excerpts from those books for this anthology. I have a book of translations of the French Poet Paul Eluard currently in consideration, and a chapbook called "Reflections in the Time of Trumpius Maximus." I offer writing workshops on Zoom, as well as "creativity sessions" using ekphrastic (visual art) prompting which is now ongoing.

I am also a classical guitarist. Pre-COVID-19, I performed at poetry readings, art openings, and restaurants, weddings and parties – a collage style mix of classical, samba, and jazz. More information about my books and music are on my website, **www.poetwithguitar.com**.

Additionally, I am the "host" of this creative gang. I

 call the meetings and act as the chair, but little more. A writers' collective is like a monastery; all the monks are equal poets.

WE ARE NOBODY

A response to an editor of the NY Times who, when asked why there was no poetry among the hundreds of books in the summer reading list, said: "Because nobody reads it."

You, nobody, reading this poem
I feel badly you're not there.
Occasionally I imagine you
Doing the dishes or watching porn,
A ghost with a joint or bottle in hand
A suicidal snob quoting Petronius.

All those books on your shelf are wanting
In the rooms of Hugo's *triggering town*.
If you're reading this poem, I pity you-
You are practically six feet in the ground.

And yet you read on, expecting something,
Something to take your invisible wings
And make them flutter with the sound of words.
We can meet secretly at midnight,
Be lovers with groping tears.

From one nobody to another-
Now is the time for our
Illicit affair.

NEW YORK, 2010

The epicenter of the world, you can be anyone
When you live there, feeling you live somewhere.
In the infested tenements or penthouse of millionaires,
You wear a voice which speaks in first person

Rushing through the turnstiles of vacant eyes
In a silence of self-absorbed realities;
Blood brother to Gomorrah, hierophant of Greece,
O city of masks, of vain electric offerings.

The bridges weave a dizzying mass of icy towers,
A density of steam and gasoline rising in the grey,
And suddenly you stand paralyzed in the rush hours
As the palpitating sirens strip you of humanity.

You are just a face in the crowded anywhere,
Seeking to be alone, to breathe a different air.

from collections: "21 Sonnets from a Time and Place," and "21 Sonnets Stirred, Not Shaken"

SALLY LIPPMAN, DISCO SALLY
(1900-1982)

I

I dreamt of you Sally, I dreamt we were doing that crazy dance
At Studio, Les Mouches, Xenon, 12 West, Infinity, in a trance
From poppers, you, an 80-year-old bubby dressed for a killing
Arriving at 3 AM when the energy was spinning.

How you swayed! I held your hand and its soft bones
Beneath your lambskin arms that swayed in a zone
Of flecks the mirrored ball reflected off your teeth;
You were lifted to the DJ who hung a flowered wreath

On your head, and with a shout you were queen of the night!
You were the angel to our faces so perfectly done,
The wet mass of shirtless skin shining in strobe lights,
Our bodies swaying with lust till the rays of the sun.

II

You told me about times in the flapper age
With the same jazzy mix of champagne and cocaine-
What a bacchanal it was then, a Jewish beauty.
What a time of saxophone bands and Gatsby parties!

In time you settled down, a hotshot lawyer, mother, wife,
A not too colorful uptown life.
Hair went brown to white, your husband died.
Years spent in sleeplessness and strife.

So you wandered the night and passed a dive
Where memories returned as you felt the vibes
From the bass shaking the foundation of the walls.
In you waltzed with curly white hair to the ball

Again to be the delirious ballerina,
Waving your arms in celebration of hysteria,
Letting your body loose with the screaming savages
Of youth, madness and dervishes of ecstasy.

O the Paradise Garage, the after-hour salons,
Sally, we disco danced lifetimes ago, ever gone.
We were lost to Gomorrah and glittery things
In our joy and oblivion to the erotic steam.

III

You died at the end of that boogie rage;
Hundreds of us showed up, with your family amazed.
They wouldn't play your favorite songs as we asked,
But we knew your little frame held the music fast.

When you were buried in the ground, and the rabbi
Tossed the dirt over your coffin, I knew then, I
Know now, you had given the redemption of a sage,
And I would dream of you in the dawn of my old age.

from collection: "21 Poems to Dead Immortals"

DEATH DON'T YOU DARE

It is not death I fear-
I have, after all, come to terms
With nightly visits to its dreamy sidekick,
Where I have no free will.
My brain concocts a landscape
Of unfamiliar collages, unremembered;
Why should death be any different?

At my bedside is the fantastic fairy tale
I'm reading, I have a few chapters left...
And how will it all end?
Will it be bacchanal, an extravaganza?
Or philosophizing not so happily ever after?
You must agree for this alone I need to be alive.
But to die in the middle of the story,
O come on now Death, no reason for cruelty!
How could you send me into that starry oblivion
Not knowing if the magic spell was broken?

And yes, I'm off to the concert hall again
Yet another Resurrection Symphony;
I'm urgently trying to cop the magic moments,
Like passport stamps, or vouchers.
There is still space in the carry-on luggage
That I'm packing to be with me in the grave.

But also, I keep on reminding myself,
Day after day, I keep on reminding myself,
It's been 50 years since I read Rimbaud or Blake.
I must go back and have them fresh in my head
Before I'll accept anything singularly disruptive
As death.

TRUMPIUS IS MAD AGAINE

April was too cruel   he's up to fifty tweets
Before breakfast   he's a tweet machine
Sweet revenge is all that he can think

Like a medieval king he sets the stage
Pounds the desk with madness and rage
He's fed up with the phony plague

Inflated statistics   the testing obscene
The White House now in quarantine
He takes aim at his enemies

He's the brand of his own disease
An addiction to a sweet nicotine
For the morally dead and morbidly obese

Sitting by their old Victrolas
With cellphones on their lap
Petting them like purring cats

While soothsayers interpret the signs
Conspiracy   deceit   deep state crimes
Inventing truth between the lines

If he could just cut out their tongues
The scientists   the press   the scum
Forget the wacko virus   it's over and done

Why then Ile fit you. Trumpius is mad againe.
Delirious. Disorientated. Demented.
           Bullshit   bullshit   bullshit

from collection: "Reflections in the Time of Trumpius Maximus"

YOU MUST PLAY WITH THE BLOOD!

You must feel the heartbreak in the minor chord,
You must feel the urgency of perfect pitch
From a choir echoing in the catacombs,
You must praise the bees heavy with pollen
Whose buzzing is an engine of spinning wings,
You must stare into the eyes of the Odalisque,
You must embrace the lions engorged with meat
And allow the crippled vultures to eat the bones,
You must accept the cruel indifference of pain
Which screams and cries in wordless shock,
You must rejoice in lust and nakedness,
You must allow yourself to spin to samba
When the carnival passes with sordo drums,
There must be fire in your words when you speak,
You must know the joy of practice and repetition
And the physical connection between the dancer
And the sound as the musician to the instrument,
You must seek out the dragon to suck its blood
To understand the sad poetry of bird song
You must be filled with the mystery of pyramids,
You must see the moon as a flower
Each phase illuminated in a major key.

But you can't play if the metronome ticks,
No, you won't play with the blood.
Instead you will be a prisoner of time.
If you live for a past that never was
And denied yourself forbidden love,
If you can't bear to sit through Rigoletto
Or ride a bike to the strings of Pergolesi,
Don't even try to play with the blood.

from collection: "21 Poems Inspired by a Declarative Statement"

Martin L Parker

Martin is a CAD, graphic, web and font designer, as well as an aspiring artist and poet.

He has been fascinated by the many aspects of language since childhood, including the interesting variety of sounds that are used, the different ways a language's grammar can be put together, and various ways the world's writing systems can be drawn artistically.

Martin graduated from Georgetown University in 1988 with a degree in Linguistics, but eventually realized he didn't fit into a traditional academic career path, as he greatly preferred writing poetry, as well as calligraphy and other forms of visual expression, to writing papers.

Aside from focusing more on his poetry lately, and exploring ways to share it with world, Martin has been creating multilingual calligrams, or images made from words from many languages, like those you can see on his website at **www.parquillian.com**.

VICTORY

You float upon subconscious streams
though't can make it hard to breathe
when sounds of jazz inflected dreams
start t' swing on a time-warp breeze

so did the man whose prejudice
ever let you take the wheel
you standin' up by sittin' down
t' express the way you feel

in front of the stand 'round midnight time
i'd be feelin' th' invisible drizzle
us blowin' the tones of a restful rhyme
'n' then makin' them gentlemen sizzle

'n' you'd be choosin' the clearer value
o' seduction amid the tomes
near where we'd weather'd a flying tantrum
'bout a tempo wand'rin' from home

'n' we'd be checkin' out the trap
havin' 'riggled out o' class
in a room o' silently sleepin' sheaths
full o' vibrant glitterin' brass

'n' you'd be askin' "how you figger?"
while we'd fake the sounds o' seagulls
us squawkin' loudly with such vigor
spirits soarin' like the eagles

'n' i'd be checking out the rhythm
o' the congan groove you pitchin'
while hearin' your sister hammer hick'ries
get'n' 'em ready for the kitchen

'n' i'd be catchin' the patchwork play
for a greeting i'd solely witness
you laughin' at them dancin' eggs
with a passionate yen for citrus

'n' you'd be wingin' that equide sphere
that 'd act more like a football
by hangin' eerily in the air
like th' echo of a footfall

'n' now you're jammin' on that 'train
fingers jumpin' with jivin' skill
while notes of all them tunes you shared
still be slidin' through my skull

t' echo there like yours did on stage
knuckles r'apsodizin' w' speed
tho' as in rumor you submerge
t' the beat of a gallopin' steed

that rezonates in my soul, brother
i never had any truer friend
and in the memories of another
you 'll triumph in the end.

in loving memory of Victor White 1964-82

THE SMITH OF THE SMOLDERING RUNESTONE RHYMES

I have *mémoires* of verbal exchanges,
sitting in spaces of *variat* tone,
with the smoldering *rúnsteinsmiður*,
who is like the *shpirt* of stone.

Rond 25 op de klok it was,
when we would *mæta* 'mid the radiance.
The reading would *kòmanse* then as,
he'd howl *i længden* in metered cadence.

Spinning out around the *κύκλος*,
under the light of the *sĭngən* moon,
tales from the land of the rising *taiyo*,
sempre arriving much too soon.

Asking things like *"goomzigahm?"*
in his own ancestral *linguam*.
Humbly conversing with *khambroeng* grace,
in the *yŭ* of the middle kingdom.

Setting ablaze *thi'ywe'* from *Bemá*,
releasing a less than *thayathàw* taste.
Accepting a well-interpreted *pakyét*,
obtained at a *moskovskiy* stall in haste.

Weaving a *gréasáin* with silver threads,
which from a *cidade sagrada* were springing,
in waning hours of the very *gishér*,
we'd missed our *megobrebi*'s singing.

Feeling effects of *shlofloz* nights,
from staying up *shpeyt* after multiple coffees.
Grabbing a bite of *pastırma* on rye,
then *shlep*ping it back to the *tsaytung* office,

Typing a *pismo* in *kirillítsa,*
pecking the *Tasten* with trembling hands,
Including a mark from the *duka* of *Yawa,*
stocked with *iincwadi* from *yeAfrika* lands.

Accosting *sarang* on Manhattan *kado,*
to grow his *gibon* grasp of Korean,
while *xödl*ing at the veritable borders,
that verge upon that *đa-ngôn-ngữ* scene.

Talking on *bhāṣalu* newly endeavored,
we'd *mintza* by way of the *telepon* line,
discussing the literal art of *aksara,*
wandering the *dvipa*'s in his mind.

Holding court in an *ásude* armchair,
in Point *enSalada*'s musical maze.
Rings of *dukhán* there slowly fading,
into a *sötét* jazz-hued haze.

These *muistoja* of mine will always be humming,
amid the *sayong* of the *velik* unknown,
e'en if the *ŝanco* is ne'er forthcoming,
to read the *runor* carved on his stone.

in loving memory of Michael Petriano

GLOSSARY FOR *"THE SMITH..."*

mémoires = memories (French)
variat = various (Romanian)
rúnsteinsmiður = runestonesmith (Icelandic)
shpirt = spirit (Albanian)
rond 25 op de klok = 'round 25 o'clock (Dutch)
mæta = meet (AngloSaxon)
kòmanse = begin (Kweyòl)
i længden = at length (Danish)

κύκλος = circle (Greek)
sĭngən = silver (Thai)
taiyo = sun (Japanese)
sempre = always (Italian)

goomzigahm? = what's your name? (Sicilian)
linguam = language (Latin)
khambroeng = effortless (Khmer)
yǔ = language (Chinese)

thi'ywe' = leaves, *Bemá* = Burma, *thayathàw* = pleasant
      (Burmese)
pakyét = pack, *moskovskiy* = Moscow (Russian)

gréasáin = web (Irish)
cidade sagrada = sacred city (Portuguese)
gisher = night (Armenian)
megobrebi = brothers (Georgian)

shlofloz = sleepless, *shpeyt* = late (Yiddish)
pastırma = pastrami (Turkish)
shlep = drag, *tsaytung* = *newspaper* (Yiddish)

písmo = letter, *kirillítsa* = Cyrillic script (Russian)
Tasten = keys (German)
duka = store, shop (kiSwahili)
Yawa = abundance (Hausa), name of a bookshop in
     Adams Morgan DC at one time
iincwadi = books (isiXhosa)
yeAfrika = African (Amharic)

sarang = people, *kado* = streets, *gibon* = basic (Korean)
xödl = work (Mongolian)
đa-ngôn-ngữ = multilingual (Vietnamese)

bhāṣalu = languages (Telugu)
mintza = speak (Basque)
telepon = telephone (Tagalog)
aksara = letters (Javanese,Indonesian)
dvipa = continent, island (Hindi)

ásude = *comfortable* (Persian)
ensalada = (&)Salad (Spanish, mutual friend's nickname,
as is *Point*)
dukhán = smoke (Arabic)
sötét = murky (Hungarian)

muistoja = memories (Finnish)
sayong = mist (Balinese)
velik = great (Slovenian)
ŝanco = chance (Esperanto)
runor = runes (Swedish)

SILVER THREADS

silver threads
from woven webs
form the soft cloth
of many colored robes
that spin round my mind
in the mi(d)st of the night
while crimson-etched orbs
of wonderous white
fill diamonds of (f)light
that sparkle and start
at thunderous sounds
which crystal distorts

and the wind keeps whispering

HIGH RISING MOON CHILD

i kept my innermost fears at bay
and sat by you on the bus that day
drawn in so close by cursive curls
your name inscribed in wax bright blue
that echoed tales of hunter girls
seen high on hills beneath the moon
entranced by those sweet lines you drew
i knew of no one else my age
in gardens where we'd head for class
beyond the roads that bus would roam
with passion for the forms that words
could take when they in groups entwine
with loops that freely fall and rise
in rolling rows of words we'd weave
within the plane - a snow white page
we laid at random on the glass
that made a table in your home
just down the hill from that of mine
where we would spend an afternoon
creating worlds from swirls that gleam
and handdrawn lines that fly like birds
or rainbows arching through the skies

until your mom said it's time to leave
and off you'd fade like a moonlit dream

for Cynthia High

SHY HUNTRESS

the colors in your satin dress
would mesmerize my naked eyes
when waiting in the line to leave
and let the hunt begin

leader of the pack of girls
chasing bobby round the grounds
with that wistful wolfish grin
and eyes of crystal blue

you trying hard to no avail
to plant a peck upon his cheek
as all the boys would do their best
to make sure that you fail

one day i caught you all alone
and dared invite you to my home
for milk and cookies mother made
you said you'd love to go

but owing to the fear of eyes
who might our very movements spy
you did aver you must decline
for fear you would be teased

EVENING OF ECHOES

i saw punks driving by in a silver volvo
as a guy struggled to put his eye back in
  and the lady said she'd left coins in her room
    fran said she'd checked the drawers and everything
  where she couldn't stay tonight
i want it now he yelled at the nervous man
  she had lots and lots and lots of money
the voices echoed from the statuary corners
there were no lights where they were going
  but the banks just wouldn't take her checks
the shadows were moving
the flowers were firmly bolted shut
  and tomorrow was may
hawaiian rings hummed at a crossing round midnight
  so she'd be getting a whole bunch more
and the broken bits of raw spaghetti
fell slowly from my hand

CATARACTS
(WATERFALL VISIONS)

gathering galaxies float by my view
showing the heavens inverted in hue
wandering pathways that cover the sky
shifting my sight through a humorous eye

as vehicles manifest out of the mist
their multifaceted lights insist
on spraying fractal florals around
like distal discs of scintillant sound

with filters scattered 'cross either eye
and visions of waterfalls rippling by
like curving trails of rising steam
or wavering borders as in a dream

sometimes in the glow of the darkening sky
i feel more blessed than hindered by
the swirling patterns and colored screens
and cataracts that cause these scenes

Rebecca Wener

Rebecca Wener is a 33-year-old global health professional, working at an NGO in the Silver Spring, Maryland area. Her poems have appeared in *Beyond Words* and *Poetry Quarterly*.

QUARANTINE
(WHEN YOU ARE ALREADY LONELY)

The morning sunlight through the slats
makes its slow honey roll across the room.

I can smell myself, only myself,
my hands and my sweat,
mine are the only hands that have been here today.

No change from yesterday.

You are the only one who ever asks,
about my hands,
my sweat,
my day.

I can hear you, on the other side of the wall,
going about your morning.

I can't hear myself, not any longer. I've gotten too loud.
Or has the world become so silent?

Please be so good as to send me a message,
whenever you happen to see this.

Tell me that this too shall pass. (*It never does.*)
Tell me that the love song of the morning,
the sun, the crowds, and lines for coffee,
will play once more, and this time
I will finally learn to hear it.

MARK THIS ONE DOWN:

Mark this one down against
the soft green sprawl of a summer afternoon:

You and me and a bottle of Bourbon
and the whole world just beyond our fingertips,
but never close enough to grasp.

We laugh ourselves silly and drink ourselves sick,
then together we make a machine with our bodies
that has never yet been seen
in the light of an impassive sun.

But you are not a mechanic
and I've never met an engine that I did not break
and all too soon the sun comes down,
smashing through the soft green silence of the day
saving me from you and you from me
and both of us from living too long inside a dream.

TOO MANY TRUTHS
(AN ELEGY FOR SEAN SPICER'S CAREER, DIGNITY AND SOUL)

Too many times you let the right words
fester in the shivering silence
that trails the phone call,
that drapes the press room
after the herd has stormed away
in search of greener targets.

The saddest truth of the moment
is the shame you carry with you,
liver heavy, spleen engorged,
regret, a toxic flush
spilled across your cheeks.

We all can see it.
All those truths you left unsaid.

Everybody knows
what stains look like,
even when they pretend to look away.

Your truth is an insect.
Praying mantis green, and
clinging tight to the bushes,
as if you think that they alone can save you.

Vadim Kagan

Vadim Kagan writes poetry and prose in English, Russian and, occasionally, in a combination of both. Vadim's poems, bringing together traditions of Russian and English metered verse, have been put to music and performed by local and international artists.

Vadim lives in Bethesda, MD, where he runs an AI (Artificial Intelligence) company providing advanced technology capabilities to Fortune 500 companies  and government agencies. His professional publications cover a range of AI subjects and include the book *Sentiment Analysis for PTSD Signals* (Springer).

DRAWING THE RAIN

I'm drawing the rain. Light dissolving to shadows,
Lines flowing to shades, white transforming to grey.
I'm drawing the rain – gushing gutters, umbrellas,
The clouds and the pavement connected by spray,
Hats, coats and boots, windows shuttered and misted,
The town reborn by reflections and sheen,
The things that I wasn't aware existed,
I'm drawing the rain that I'm drowning in.

"Tallinn" by Juliya Ivanilova. Reproduced with the artist's permission.

DAISIES

Who writes of daisies at a time like this,
When worlds are quickly coming to an end,
When state of fear replaced the state of bliss?
But daisies are still beautiful, my friend,
And golden is the dandelion wine.

Who writes of daisies as we lose the fight,
When thousands and thousands are dead,
When states are failing, falling left and right?
But daisies are still beautiful, my friend,
And golden is the dandelion wine.

Who writes of daisies when we live online,
And die with cabin fever taking hold,
But golden is the dandelion wine
And daisies are as beautiful as ever —
Let's write of daisies. They might save the world.

ZEITNOT

There is no time. No time is left at all,
No days are left, no weeks, no months, no seasons,
And all the clocks have stopped without a reason.
The chimes are silent. Bells no longer toll.

There is no time where time forever was,
No sand, no springs, no batteries, no water;
All hands have stopped at midnight and a quarter,
The gears are clenched in dusty rusting jaws.

There is no time. We spent it all, it seems,
And we have missed that moment, one and only,
When we were neither desperate nor lonely
And in control of destinies and dreams.

There is no time. No time to say goodbye,
To kiss the tears off long forgotten lashes,
All that is left are slowly cooling ashes.
There is no time. There is no time. No ti…

I HATE NY

I hate New York. I deeply hate New York,
Where gods and people mingle and despair;
And we would never ever travel there
If it were not for masochism of work.
You never-sated, sleepless angry beast,
Your pungent smell is always in the air -
A mix of charging bull and roaring bear,
The one and only Gotham of the east.

New York, I hate you. You just never stop;
You justify whatever price we pay you
By golden dreams that slowly fade to black.
You take us from the bottom to the top,
And dump us when we have no further value.
Good-bye, New York. I hate you. I'll be back.

"Verticals" by Michael Taratuta. Reproduced with the author's permission.

L&B 2.1

Love and beauty tried to save the world,
Love and beauty failed and had to leave,
Love and beauty, hopelessly naive
Could not stop the changes that unfurled.

Love and beauty chose a foreign land,
Love and beauty learned to surf and sail,
Love and beauty drank to no avail
Waiting for the world to sigh and end.

Love and beauty loved each other, but
Love and beauty hated getting old;
Love and beauty split the pot of gold
And agreed that their ties were cut.

Love applied to change its name to Hate,
Beauty launched a line of fancy creams;
Not concerned with followers and dreams,
Both of them are now doing great.

STARS

Let me see the stars
In your eyes tonight
Let this night be ours
Till the morning light
Let me touch your hair
Let me smell your skin
Let me just be there
If you let me in

Let me make you smile
Let me make you sigh
If you let me, I'll
Never ask you why
Moon is getting low
Night is getting gray
Please don't make me go
Let me stay the day

Let me see the sun
On your skin so pale
Let us be as one
Let us both exhale
Let me hold you tight
Let me kiss you slow
Let me, and you might
Never let me go

HOW OFTEN

How often those that help us aren't the ones
That we've been praying to - but other gods and angels
Who hear our prayers in reruns
And, out of curiosity or anger
Or love
Come from above
To Earth moonlit and glowing
To give us what, without really knowing,
We asked them for;
In their bliss divine,
They play with our words
Until they shine
Like bright and hot but very distant suns.
How often those that help us aren't the ones.

Zebra Black

My poems remain explorations of the subconscious erotic. They are lunar anamorphic streams of consciousness from the deep chaotic subterranean glitz of transgressive impulses we all share, those dark secrets we keep from ourselves.

THE FUKFU BAR SHABARI STAR...
ERO GURO

tattooed girl
hello kitty
in need of a purge
she cums first
in the whip me
with a wet noodle
pain Olympics

her fruit launcher
like a summer papaya
pussy gush
kissey squirts
candy crush
all gobbledygoo
and lickyfu

ooow she swayed
to the whip back crack
her torso bent
heaven sent

dipped in hot pot
and laughing lady sauce
she squealed
for
bok choy
eel cock
and slippy toy

butt buttered waffles
and gummy worms
lime and cherry dicks
with candy sperms

you can find her
in the bend over den
eating puffer fish
so very Zen

toes gooey wet
spread on a cot
oh so high
suck and squat
shibari baby
tied in a knot

cunt bobba bubble
and chrysanthemum tea
nut scented black beer
and milk pearl pee

it's the end of the line
ready to dine
get the gag
flex the spine

face to the ground
feet to the sky
held like a dove
cunts splash cry

DISTURBING FLESHY TEXT

body genre
at a carnal address
sensory and sensuous effects
materiality
digital images
anthropology of desire

she tied a knot around his cock
a wedding band made of shoelaces
for the art of tongue and suck
driving it in her mouth
back and forth
like a shift stick

Videodrome
for the retina
a puzzlement and fascination
haptic screen of fiction

adventure of being pinned down
an unpremeditated punctum

the stadium of desire
a shop window
banality transcending banality
the literal transformed
into the erotic

girl in a suitcase
with a hole to fuck
a treasure chest
the leaky boundaries of erotica

I packed her up
limbless and threw
her on the bed
and with tender kisses
of endless
wet permutations
banged
three oozing holes
into oblivion

gender
age play
bimbo class
weird ethnicity
from Timbuktu
racially motivated lust for a
conveyance of
fleshy intensities

a big cock dips
a tender dimple

the violence of it
a preemptive strike
for everything imaginable
in the cosmos
finer than frog fur

oh happy boner
a suicide orgasm
at the computer screen

River Styx of flames

GUILLOTINE

diaphanous girl
a headless masquerade
her black lipstick and shivering pearls
giggle like earthquake chandeliers

festooned buttocks
curves a lyrical hell of desire

pocket eyes
dead suns
aloof
yield vacant split azure vault
a fetish horror
zoomorphic and decapitated

a thrilled non compos mentis
her mouth widens
like a line turning into a circle
turning into a jagged city
of twining red wet mayhem

fish head stare
and toothy kisses
on red abdomen posy hook
jutting her spine for sadistic fires
she rolls her velvet thighs
wriggling
a wrench
and twitch
a mad headless lunar sputnik
circumambulates spit tongue sputum

she is the eye in the sky of eternal night
her spirit impaled upon
torrential mountain libidos
impaled on a wildlife park of cocks

wet fingering a basket of skulls
she nestled
her depraved tilted crown
lilting onto the stained guillotine

saying come on
i can hardly wait to get started
make me the ghastly queen
goddess of the witching hour
bone blood
and black glitter dead of night

S & M

There is a part of us
that isn't quite alive

until hollow-starved lunacy is sated

while showing the bright side
her hidden darkness emerged
when i tricked her into hurting herself

she would say come on trick me, trick me, trick me
and i would tell her
Count Dragool with bloody tube fingers
would take her slow
if she hit herself hard across the mouth
and she would scream to Eden
bash mashley thrash me
i want the men with red tridents
and ding dong tails too
while she watched my eyes
like surveillance drones
as if a great confederation of cocks
marched towards her

certainly not painless
but the pain of an addict
who knows all too well the pleasure of the needle
first the little sting and then the great ooooow

she is butter on the stove
i'm the rare drug
a Dodo bird beaking flesh
a cold hard penetration

she a yielding intricacy of complications
a bald Rapunzel
feeling under-abused till now
with black crow lips and bangled earrings
like a long jangling math problem that ends
with a big O

O popping blood berries
like pink flower hysterical nipples
shooting bullets from tattooed
hip belted pistols
on a singing red bed

her limbs a yawing stretch
a torn zipper
being yanked up and down
a frenzy of crying blasphemies and raw kisses
dancing the bend over
on knotted knees
incised a writhing dance cha cha

creel of blood
cha cha cha

THE SAINT OF SADISM

flex and perspire my darling
would you mind a small suffering for craven kisses
to have your dark fig anus and drenching vulva
stroked with a tickling finger lingering
and strong hands around your sweetly curved throat
that shunt the breath
to yield willingly for sharp-toothed nibbles with surprise
tongue whipping?

will you present your soft belly and cupping breasts
for dark cruelties that excite beyond tabulation
will you present yourself with smiles
and goddess leg show
sobbing for feral pink spires gleaming
while quivering thighs
turn hot red from the slap of the leather strap splitting
stings?

will tears of love
mix in wild berry utterance
and flashing spitfire's tongue?

are you made for this?
your every whimper an invitation
like an open pink gate
do you need the saint of dark desires to rescue you
from banal dim-witted all-american in-and-out?

do you need to drown in oceanic wave tsunamis
of hot butter fuck glitter, blood flooding gasms
and tender aftercare?

my wish
that you shimmer like silver
possessed
by the saint of sadism
popes of eros
who fill you with the milk of the moon
all stars that melt you into the depths of paradise

and that this dark ecstasy
is the only suffering you will ever know

LEAVING A REVIEW ON AMAZON

If you enjoyed this book, please consider leaving a review on Amazon. It's is easy and it helps books get noticed! Why? When Amazon ranks a book, the ranking is based on the volume of purchases of the book and the number of reviews left by readers on the book's review page. More reviews will get the book noticed and will create trust with potential buyers looking to purchase the book.

- Go to **www.Amazon.com**
- Log in to your account
- Click on "Orders" in the top menu
- Find your order placed for *iNK BLOTS, Vol. 1*
- At the right, click on "Write a Product Review"
- Simply leave a review and click "Submit"

If the book was a gift and you did not purchase it, you can still submit a review if you have an Amazon-buying history.

- Go to **www.Amazon.com**
- Find the Amazon book page for *iNK BLOTS, Vol. 1*
- Scroll down to "Review This Product"
- Simply leave a review and click "Submit"

www.ingramcontent.com/pod-product-compliance
Lightning Source LLC
Chambersburg PA
CBHW030604130626
46552CB00006B/2657